Windsurfing

The World's Windiest Water Sport Spots and Techniques

by Paul Mason

CAPSTONE PRESS
a capstone imprint

Edge Books are published by
Capstone Press, a Capstone imprint,
151 Good Counsel Drive, P.O. Box 669,
Mankato, Minnesota 56002.
www.capstonepub.com

First published 2011
Copyright © 2011 A & C Black
Publishers Limited

Produced for A & C Black by
Monkey Puzzle Media Ltd,
48 York Avenue,
Hove BN3 1PJ, UK

032010
005746ACF10

The right of Paul Mason to be identified as
the author of this Work has been asserted by
him in accordance with the Copyright, Designs,
and Patents Act 1988.

Library of Congress Cataloging-in-Publication
Data
Mason, Paul, 1967-
  Windsurfing: the World's Windiest Water
  Sport Spots and Techniques / by Paul Mason.
  p. cm. -- (Passport to World Sports)
  Includes bibliographical references and index.
  ISBN 978-1-4296-5502-6 (library binding)
  1. Windsurfing--Juvenile literature. I. Title.
  II. Series.

GV811.63.W56M37 2011
796.3'3--dc22

2010014064

Editor: Dan Rogers
Design: Mayer Media Ltd
Picture research: Lynda Lines

This book is produced using paper that
is made from wood grown in managed,
sustainable forests. It is natural, renewable,
and recyclable. The logging and manufacturing
processes conform to the environmental
regulations of the country of origin.

Picture acknowledgements
Action Images pp. 1 (Benjamin Thouard/DPPI),
4 (Benjamin Thouard/DPPI), 6 (Huber Images/
Zumapress.com), 11 (Benjamin Thouard/DPPI),
23 (Benjamin Thouard/DPPI), 28 (Benjamin
Thouard/DPPI), 29 (Benjamin Thouard/DPPI);
Alamy pp. 5 (Nicholas Pitt), 7 (Buzz Pictures),
9 (Stephen Bardens), 10 (Carrie Bond), 15
(Buzz Pictures), 19 (Bjorn Svensson), 22 (Alan
Campbell), 24 bottom (Picture Contact); Funsurf
p. 16; Getty Images pp. 20 (Richard Hallman),
26, 27; Brian Keels p. 14 middle; Danielle Lucas
p. 25; MPM Images pp. 12, 13; No Zomi p. 14
bottom; Photolibrary pp. 17 (Erik Aeder), 18
(Ingolf Pompe/LOOK-foto), 21 (Fotosearch
Value); Pueblo Project p. 8; Wikimedia
Commons pp. 14 top, 24 top. Compass rose
artwork on front cover and inside pages by
iStockphoto. Map artwork by MPM Images.

The front cover shows a windsurfer in action
at the Colombia River Gorge (Corbis/Richard
Hallman/Aurora).

Every effort has been made to contact copyright
holders of material reproduced in this book.
Any omissions will be rectified in subsequent
printings if notice is given to the publishers.

SAFETY ADVICE

Don't attempt any of the
activities or techniques
in this book without the
guidance of a qualified
windsurfing instructor.

CONTENTS

It's a Wet and Windy World   4

Lake Garda   6

Cabarete   8

Poole Harbour   10

The Speed World Cup   12

Lake Arenal   14

Dahab   16

El Yaque   18

The Gorge   20

Tarifa   22

Essaouira   24

Tiree Wave Classic   26

Ho'okipa   28

Glossary   30

Finding out More   31

Index   32

It's a Wet and Windy World

You're skimming across the tops of the white-capped waves, your feet safely planted on the **deck** of the windsurfing board. The tail chatters as you race along, spray hitting you in the face. The wind gusts, and you do a little jump, land, and zoom onward. If that sounds fun, it's time for you to get into windsurfing.

Is it a bird? Is it a plane? No—it's an all-action wave-riding windsurfer.

DREAM TICKET

Imagine you have a dream ticket that could take you windsurfing anywhere you wanted, any time! Where should you go? Where are the world's best windsurfing spots for beginners, intermediate sailors, and experts? This book can help you decide the places that should be on your list.

Technical: Conditions and equipment

Windsurfing equipment is very specialized. There are windsurfing boards, sails, and other equipment for light winds, stronger winds above about 15.5 miles per hour (25 kilometers per hour), and different kinds of windsurfing.

Light winds:

• Boards tend to be bigger, with a volume of 35.7–52.8 gallons (135–200 liters). They float when you stand on them.

• Sails are small—about 43 square feet (4 square meters)—for beginners, making them easy to control.

• Intermediate sailors and experts use large sails of 64.6–107.6 square feet (6–10 square meters), to catch more wind and go faster.

Strong winds:

• Boards are smaller and more maneuverable, with a volume of 15.9–29.1 gallons (60–110 liters).

• The boards sink below the surface if you stand on them and are sometimes called "sinkers."

• Sails range from 64.6 square feet (6 square meters) in medium-strength winds to 37.7 square feet (3.5 square meters) in the highest winds.

Specialist equipment:

• Wave **sailors** use short, wider boards, and specially designed sails.

• Slalom and speed sailors use sails shaped to catch as much wind as possible. The speed sailors use narrow boards that slice through the water.

• A harness allows control of the sail in high winds.

THE SECRET LANGUAGE OF WINDSURFING

deck top of a windsurfing board
sailor someone who does windsurfing or other kinds of sailing
kook incompetent person

HINTS AND TIPS

Of course, when you get to the world's best windsurfing spots, you'll need to be sure you know what you're doing. No one wants to look like a **kook**! So we tell you what each windsurfing location is like and the kind of equipment you'll need. We also have tips from local sailors and advice on technique. This book is your passport to the windsurfing world!

Rows of different boards ready for people to use in a variety of conditions

Lake Garda

There can't be many places where you can windsurf in warm sunshine, then look up to see snowcapped mountains towering above you. Lake Garda is one of them. Its beautiful location, reliable wind, and great facilities attract windsurfers from all over the world.

WHY LAKE GARDA?

Lake Garda is over 37 miles (60 kilometers) long and over 9 miles (15 kilometers) wide at its biggest parts. The coast is made up of a series of beaches, rocky platforms, and cliff faces. There is somewhere here for every kind of windsurfer— from beginners looking for a calm lagoon to do some **flat-water sailing** to experts who want high winds, open water, and waves.

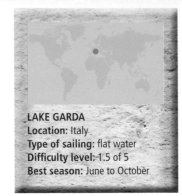

LAKE GARDA
Location: Italy
Type of sailing: flat water
Difficulty level: 1.5 of 5
Best season: June to October

Windsurfing on the spectacular Lake Garda in Italy

THE SECRET LANGUAGE OF WINDSURFING

flat-water sailing windsurfing on a lake or ocean with little or no waves

mast foot attachment between the mast and the deck

Tip from a Local
In July and August, the lake water is sometimes warm enough for sailing without a wetsuit—but the rest of the year, you do need one.

WHEN ARE CONDITIONS BEST?

Beginners: In general, winds are lighter mid-morning, so this is the best time for beginners. The bay at Torbole, at the northern end of the lake, is a good place for complete beginners.

Intermediate sailors: In the early afternoon, the Ora wind blows from the south at 15–20 miles per hour (about 25–35 kilometers per hour), making ideal conditions for intermediates.

Experts: Very early in the morning, the Vento wind from the north can reach over 37.3 miles per hour (60 kilometers per hour)—hard work even for expert sailors.

If you like Lake Garda ...
you could also try:
• Forest Beach Park, Illinois
It has a real big-lake feel.

TECHNIQUE
Understanding the wind

The wind and sail together can be used to figure out which direction the wind is coming from. Then, by moving the sail, the sailor can change the direction in which the board is facing.

1. Hold the sail out of the water so that it can float free in the air. With one foot on either side of the **mast foot**, hold the mast straight upright. The board will swing around so that the wind is right behind you.

2. Lean the mast and sail backward, toward the tail of the board. The board will swing round so that its nose is pointing into the wind. The farther back the mast leans, the more into the wind the board will point.

3. Lean the mast forward, toward the nose of the board. The board will move around so that its tail is pointing toward the wind.

A wobbly-looking beginner takes her first try at windsurfing. At least the water looks warm, for when she falls in.

Cabarete

The Caribbean has a lot to offer windsurfers. In particular, the warm water and all-year sunny weather make the region very popular with sailors from colder countries. During the official hurricane season from June to October, winds can reach 75 miles per hour (120 kilometers per hour) or more. Fortunately, this doesn't happen very often.

WHY CABARETE?

Cabarete is one of the most popular windsurfing destinations in the Caribbean Sea. All year round, strong winds blow from the east. Beginners and intermediate sailors are sheltered from waves by a reef, which forms the outer edge of a large lagoon. The reef is where expert sailors go for the thrill of **wave sailing**.

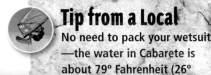

Tip from a Local

No need to pack your wetsuit —the water in Cabarete is about 79° Fahrenheit (26° Celsius) all year round.

If you like Cabarete ...

you could also try:
• Kilifi, Kenya
There's warm water, and the conditions are varied.

The shallow lagoon at Cabarete is popular with top sailors who want to practice tricks on flat water.

WHEN ARE CONDITIONS BEST?

Beginners: Winds are lighter in the morning, when beginners tend to stick to the sheltered waters inside the reef. Here they can practice in safe sight of the rescue boat.

Intermediate sailors: Around lunchtime the wind starts to pick up, and the intermediates head out onto the water.

Experts: By about 4 p.m. the wind is at its strongest. Expert sailors head out to the reef for some wave-sailing practice.

THE SECRET LANGUAGE OF WINDSURFING

wave sailing windsurfing on rough water, particularly on ocean waves

uphaul rope attached to boom, used to pull sail from water

boom rail attached to the mast, which the sailor holds on to

Once the sail starts to slide out of the water like this, the hard work is done.

SKILL
Hauling up the sail

Learning to pull up the sail is one of the first things windsurfers have to learn. There's a knack to it: If it's hard work, you're not doing it right!

1. With one foot on either side of the mast foot, grab hold of the **uphaul** rope.

2. Put your weight on the rope, bending your knees and keeping your arms and back straight. There is no need to pull—just let your weight do the work.

3. As the sail begins to slide out of the water, start to stand up straighter.

4. Leave the far corner of the sail in the water until you are standing up and have your balance.

5. Pull the sail entirely from the water and put your hands on the **boom**, ready to pull the far end of the sail inward.

Poole Harbour

On a warm summer day, with the pine trees rustling in the wind and the water gleaming blue, Poole Harbour looks more like the Mediterranean Sea than the south coast of England. The area is a hotbed of windsurfing, **kitesurfing**, and surfing, so there's always someone around to talk to (and maybe get some advice from).

POOLE HARBOUR
Location: Dorset, England
Type of sailing: flat water
Difficulty level: 1 of 5
Best season: May to October

THE SECRET LANGUAGE OF WINDSURFING

kitesurfing water sport powered by a kite, with the sailor standing on a small, surfboard-like board

rig sail, mast, and boom together

blasting windsurfing at maximum speed

WHY POOLE HARBOUR?

Poole Harbour is one of the best spots anywhere in the world for beginners to practice. The harbor is completely sheltered from the ocean, and large areas are only knee-deep. If you fall off, it's easy to climb right back on! This is the second-largest natural harbor in the world, so there are plenty of islands and beaches to explore.

These sailors have hopped across to Sandbanks for a little open-ocean sailing.

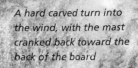
A hard carved turn into the wind, with the mast cranked back toward the back of the board

If you like Poole Harbour ...
you could also try:
• Lesvos, Greece
Which has great conditions for beginners.

Tip from a Local
In the middle of Poole Harbour is Brownsea Island. It's famous as a bird sanctuary, and as one of the last places in England where red squirrels survive.

TECHNIQUE
Steering

Poole Harbour, with its moored boats, buoys, and other watercraft zipping about, is a perfect place to practice your steering. (Remember, if it looks like you're going to hit something, drop the sail and stop before it's too late.)

• To steer straight across the wind, the mast needs to be upright and the sail pulled in.

• To steer away from the wind (which sailors call "downwind"), lean the whole **rig** forward. Done quickly, this will lead to a tight turn. Done slowly, the turn will be long and drawn out.

• To steer into the wind, or "upwind," lean the rig backward, toward the tail of the board.

WHEN ARE CONDITIONS BEST?
Beginners and intermediate sailors: Poole Harbour isn't usually too windy for beginners, but the breeze often picks up in the afternoon. This makes it harder for complete beginners to steer around the moored boats— but more fun for intermediates.

Experts: Experts will enjoy **blasting** across the harbor at high speed. Or they can do some wave sailing on the ocean off Sandbanks Beach.

11

The Speed World Cup

Imagine a windsurfer traveling so quickly it could overtake traffic in the slow lane. At a Speed World Cup event, that's just what you can see. Across Europe in the spring and summer, there's a good chance to see some of the fastest sailors in the world up close, at a series of contests called the Speed World Cup.

THE SPEED WORLD CUP
Location: worldwide
Type of sailing: speed
Difficulty level: 5 of 5
Best season: all year

SPEED-SAILING CONTESTS

The Speed World Cup is open to all kinds of sail-powered craft. As well as windsurfers, there are sailboats and kitesurfers. The racers are timed over a straight-line, 1,640-foot (500-meter) long course and can reach speeds of over 55 miles per hour (about 90 kilometers per hour). In windsurfing, the sailors use huge sails of 107.6 square feet (10 square meters) and narrow boards.

Great technique for getting maximum speed from a board: The gap between the foot of the sail and the deck is closed, and the back edge of the rig is pulled right in.

GBR 708

FANATIC

Finian Maynard, at one time the world's fastest windsurfer, in training for a speed-sailing event

Speed Records

In the 1980s and 1990s, windsurfers were among the fastest sailcraft on the water. Recently, both sailboats and kitesurfers have been faster. In 2009, the sailboat *Hydroptère* managed a speed of 51.36 knots, or 59.10 miles per hour (95.11 kilometers per hour). At that time, the three fastest windsurfers ever were:

1. Antoine Albeau (France)   49.09 knots (56.49 miles per hour or 90.91 kilometers per hour)

2. Finian Maynard (British Virgin Islands)   48.70 knots (56.04 miles per hour or 90.19 kilometers per hour)

3. Patrik Diethelm (Italy)   46.57 knots (53.59 miles per hour or 86.25 kilometers per)

These world records were all set on a 1,640-foot (500-meter) course at the French town of Saintes-Maries-de-la-Mer. The town has a strip of water known as "The French Trench," which was specially built for speed sailing on a windsurfer.

The Speed World Cup usually starts in late March, in France. Then it moves around to other countries in Europe: Sweden, Greece, Germany, Austria, the United Kingdom, Holland, and Ireland. You can track down events through the Speed World Cup website at www.speedworldcup.com.

SPEED-SAILING CENTRAL

The top locations for speed sailing world records are Saintes-Maries-de-la-Mer in France and Namibia, southern Africa. The Namibia records have been set either at the Lüderitz Speed Challenge in the town of Lüderitz, or at Walvis Bay Speed Week.

Lake Arenal

Lake Arenal must be one of the world's most unusual windsurfing locations. It was created when a hydroelectric dam was built in 1973. The lake is so big that it took three years to fill up. Looming over one end is a huge volcano—which can sometimes be heard rumbling and grumbling in the background.

LAKE ARENAL
Location: Costa Rica
Type of sailing: flat water, some small waves
Difficulty level: 2 of 5
Best season: all year

Tip from a Local

If it rains, it usually rains harder on the north side of the lake—so if you like the sunshine, stay on the south shore.

Lake Arenal's constant winds make it a great place for racing around doing jumps.

WHY LAKE ARENAL?

The lake covers 32.8 square miles (85 square kilometers), so somewhere on its shores there are conditions to suit everyone. For beginners, there are sheltered areas for practicing hauling up the sail, plus turning around by **tacking** or **jibing**. For more experienced sailors, the wind blows stronger farther out on the lake. On strong-wind days, there are even small waves for practicing jumps.

If you like Lake Arenal ...

you could also try:
• Foca, Turkey
It has sheltered areas for practice.

WHEN ARE CONDITIONS BEST?

Beginners: From May to October, there are lighter winds that are ideal for beginners. Windy days are less common, but if the wind drops off completely, you can always visit the volcano. It's advertised as being "90 percent safe"!

Intermediate sailors and experts: The lake is windiest from November to April, and this is when more experienced sailors head for Lake Arenal. On a few days a year the wind gets over 50 miles per hour (80 kilometers per hour). Only the real experts head out when this happens.

THE SECRET LANGUAGE OF WINDSURFING

tack turn with the nose of the board into the wind

jibe turn with the nose of the board away from the wind

About a third of the way through a tack, this sailor is about to step around the mast and change direction.

SKILL
Turning around

Turning around, so that you can get back to shore, is one of the most crucial skills in windsurfing, for obvious reasons. The easiest way to turn the board around is to tack.

1. Lean the mast backward, so that the board heads up into the wind.

2. Step your front foot in front of the mast and bring your hands to the front of the boom.

3. Reach around the mast with your rear hand, to grip the boom on the other side of the sail.

4. Step around the mast and bring your other hand (which is now your rear hand) around, too.

5. Lean the sail forward so that the wind pulls the board right around. Sail away with a smile.

Dahab

If you asked most windsurfers to describe their perfect sailing spot, they'd probably say:

- consistent winds of about 15 to 20 miles per hour (about 25 to 30 kilometers per hour)
- warm air and sea temperatures
- a variety of types of sailing, including flat water and wave sailing.

Dahab has all three of these.

DAHAB
Location: Egypt
Type of sailing: flat water, small waves
Difficulty level: 2.5 of 5
Best season: all year

It might look like a crash, but it isn't. This sailor is using Dahab's constant wind to practice his wave-sailing techniques.

If you like Dahab ...
you could also try:
- Porto Heli, Greece
It's good for planing.

WHY DAHAB?

Dahab is a sheltered bay on the coast of the Red Sea. Everything about the bay seems to have been designed for windsurfing. The wind blows in a direction that makes sure anyone who gets into difficulty is simply blown to a sandy beach. In winter, European windsurfers head here for the warm water and constant winds.

Tip from a Local
Dahab's winds are strongest in summer, when the desert temperatures are highest and pull air off the sea.

WHEN ARE CONDITIONS BEST?

Beginners: The calm, shallow water of the inner bay is ideal for beginners to practice in the morning.

Intermediate sailors: Farther out in the bay it is windier, especially later in the day. Intermediates can practice their turns and try little jumps in safety.

Experts: Outside the lagoon is a reef where the waves can reach 13 feet (4 meters) high. This is where the experts head for some wave sailing.

SKILL
Planing and speed

"Planing" happens when a windsurfer is going fast enough to skim along on top of the water like a speedboat, instead of plowing through it like a canoe. Good sailors are quickly able to get their board planing:

1. At first, the board is sailing **across the wind** but not planing.

2. The sailor leans forward and angles the mast slightly forward. This steers the board downwind and gives it an extra boost of speed.

3. The extra burst of speed lifts the board on to the plane.

4. Once the board is skimming along, the sailor slowly angles the mast back, to come across the wind once more.

The board remains on the plane because it needs less power to stay on the plane than it did to start planing.

A perfect planing picture, with the board skimming along the top of the water, just the tail and fin touching the surface.

El Yaque

El Yaque is a windsurfing hotspot on the tiny Caribbean island of Margarita. During the northern winter, warm air, warm water, and a warm welcome bring windsurfers to the island from all round the world. From December until April, steady winds blow past the island and guarantee good windsurfing.

EL YAQUE
Location: Margarita Island, Venezuela
Type of sailing: flat water, wind chop
Difficulty level: 2.5 of 5
Best season: November to May

Why El Yaque?

El Yaque has a combination of lagoon sailing, where the water is rarely more than waist-deep, and open-ocean windsurfing. The water in the lagoon is so shallow that if you fall off, you can easily just jump back on the board. Farther out, the **wind chop** gives experts a chance to practice their jumps.

THE SECRET LANGUAGE OF WINDSURFING

wind chop small, peaky waves thrown up by wind
freestyle using jumps, fast turns, and spins of the sail

You can tell by the shape of the tops of the trees that the wind is blowing nicely in Margarita.

If you like El Yaque ...
you could also try:
• Cervantes, Western Australia
It has great flat-water sailing.

Using footstraps and harness

Tip from a Local
If the wind drops off, try surfing, diving, or snorkeling.

This sailor is nicely hooked in and is letting the harness lines and the footstraps take the strain.

WHEN ARE CONDITIONS BEST?

Beginners: In the morning, there are lighter winds of about 12 miles per hour (about 20 kilometers per hour), so conditions are great for beginners in the lagoon.

Intermediate sailors: Around lunchtime the wind starts to pick up and intermediates will head out onto the water. Smaller sails are needed because of the more powerful winds.

Experts: By about 3 p.m. the wind can reach 30 miles per hour (about 50 kilometers per hour). Expert sailors, riding small boards with small sails, head out on to the sea for some **freestyle** windsurfing.

In stronger winds, sailors use a harness to take some of the strain off their arms. The harness connects their body to the boom and allows them to use their body weight to balance against the sail. When using a harness, sailors also wedge their feet into the footstraps on the deck of the board.

1. Only try to hook into the harness once the board is planing.

2. Pull the boom toward you and lift your body slightly so that the harness lines hook on to the harness itself.

3. With your back knee bent, slide your front foot into the front footstrap. Then move your rear foot backward and into one of the rear footstraps.

4. Let your weight go forward into the boom, to put pressure through the mast foot. This keeps the board flat and increases speed.

The Gorge

THE GORGE
Location: Washington/Oregon
Type of sailing: all types
Difficulty level: 3 of 5
Best season: April to November

Who says you don't get waves on rivers? This sailor seems to have found one at the Colombia River Gorge.

The Gorge is a world-famous windsurfing location with a difference—it's on a river, rather than the ocean or a lake. Its full name is the Columbia River Gorge. Winds blow along the gorge past the town of Hood River. The town has become a favorite stop-off for some of the world's best windsurfers.

WHY THE GORGE?

The Gorge has every kind of sailing (apart from wave sailing on open-ocean **swells**, of course). The wind blows more strongly in some spots than others. On the same day, intermediate sailors can be blasting to and fro at Home Valley, while a few miles away the experts are jumping large waves at Swell City.

Tip from a Local

The river barges on the Columbia River can't stop very quickly. It's best to stay well away from them unless you're an expert sailor.

If you like The Gorge ...

you could also try:
• River Rhine, Germany
It offers plenty of river-sailing thrills.

About a third of the way through a carved jibe, this sailor is about to let go with his rear hand and flip the rig around.

SKILL
Carving jibes

Carved jibes are one of the techniques that mark out really good sailors. A carved jibe is one where the board makes a long, drawn-out turn without stopping planing.

1. The sailor takes his or her back foot out of the strap and turns the board downwind. It's important to keep the speed up.

2. A third of the way through the turn, the sail is out to the side as the board runs downwind. The rider's weight is in the center of the board and his or her feet are out of both footstraps.

3. Halfway through the turn, still planing, the rider lets go with his or her rear hand. The sail flips around and the rider reaches across, grabs the boom with his or her free hand, and transfers the other hand.

4. The rider then **sheets in**, gaining power as shown in the technique feature on page 17. The board should keep planing and head off in the opposite direction.

THE SECRET LANGUAGE OF WINDSURFING

swell rolling ocean waves that come into the beach in lines

sheet in pull the trailing end of the boom toward the board

WHEN ARE CONDITIONS BEST?

Beginners: The Gorge isn't ideal for complete beginners, but Home Valley in the mornings is not too windy and has calmer water.

Intermediate sailors: The area around the town of Hood River has small waves and good wind for intermediates.

Experts: It's experts-only among the big waves and strong winds of Doug's Beach, Swell City, or Rufus.

Tarifa

Tarifa sits on the very southern tip of Spain. Less than 12 miles (20 kilometers) away lies Africa's coast. When the wind comes from the south, you might hear the sound of the muezzin calling North African Muslims to their morning prayers. Mostly, though, the wind comes from the east or the west, channeled through the strip of water between Europe and Africa.

TARIFA
Location: Spain
Type of sailing: all types
Difficulty level: 3.5 of 5
Best season: all year

Tarifa is a popular spot, as this melée of windsurfers and kitesurfers shows. But there's plenty of wind and water to go around.

WHY TARIFA?

This is one of Europe's best, most popular windsurfing and kitesurfing destinations. It is almost always windy and, depending on which wind is blowing, conditions are good for different types of sailing. The Levante wind blows from the Mediterranean and brings warm air and smooth seas. The Poniente blows from the Atlantic and brings cooler air and rough seas.

Tip from a Local

The water off Tarifa is usually quite chilly, even in the middle of summer. You'll definitely need a wetsuit.

WHEN ARE CONDITIONS BEST?

Beginners: Tarifa's large, sand-bottomed bay is perfect for beginners in the morning.

Intermediate sailors: Around noon, the wind starts to pick up and intermediates head for the bay.

Experts: Expert sailors wait for the strong Levante winds, or go wave sailing when the Poniente is blowing surf in from the Atantic.

THE SECRET LANGUAGE OF WINDSURFING

sheet out release the trailing edge of the boom so that the sail catches less wind

If you like Tarifa ...

you could also try:
• Paracuru, Brazil
It has great flat-water and wave sailing.

He's looking for a safe landing—but it doesn't really seem as if there is one.

Jumps: high or long?

Nothing beats the feeling of suddenly, silently flying through the air after you've done a jump! At first, people learn two main kinds of jump:

• **Jumping high:** The sailor picks a steep section of wave to launch the jump. As the board takes off, the sailor **sheets out** the sail. The board goes steeply up into the air, then comes back down to land on its tail. It almost (but not quite) floats down using the sail as a parachute.

• **Jumping long:** The sailor sheets out the sail, then as the board goes up the ramp, he or she sheets back in. The sailor then stays sheeted in through the air. The board sails forward, almost as if it is windsurfing through thin air. Most experts sheet out slightly as they land, to avoid the risk of landing nose-first and crashing.

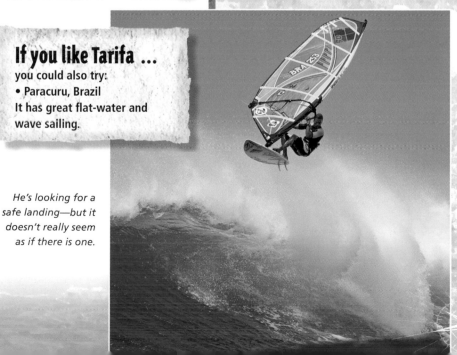

23

Essaouira

Essaouira is one of the oldest ports on Morocco's Atlantic coast. Here, traveling windsurfers get a chance to experience the ancient culture of North Africa—and some of the best windsurfing anywhere. Advanced sailors in particular flock here, because of the excellent wave sailing.

ESSAOUIRA
Location: Morocco
Type of sailing: all types
Difficulty level: 4 of 5
Best season: June to August is windiest; November to March has the biggest waves

WHY ESSAOUIRA?

Essaouira's long beach is partially sheltered from trade winds by the town. This is one of the things that make it such a great place for windsurfers. Beginners can sail in the area most protected from the wind. Experts can go farther down the bay, where the wind blows harder and the waves pick up.

The town of Essaouira blocks some wind, and provides intermediate sailors with a bit of shelter. A little farther down the coast, the sailing is for experts only.

If you like Essaouira ...
you could also try:
- Deseado Estuary, Argentina
It averages 300 windy days a year.

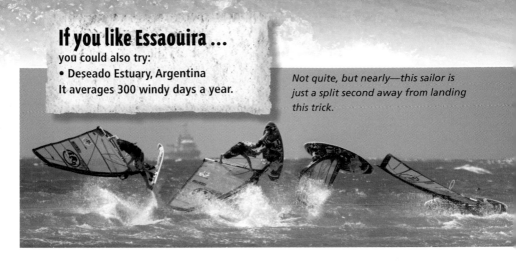

Not quite, but nearly—this sailor is just a split second away from landing this trick.

TECHNIQUE
Loops and barrel rolls

The technique that most clearly shows the difference between a good sailor and a really expert one is the loop.

- In a loop, the sailor does a jump, then flips with the board 360 degrees in the air, like a roller coaster. The board lands back on the water pointing the same way as when it started.

There are two main variations of loop: forward and backward.

- The backward loop, which used to be called a "barrel roll," is the easier of the two—although few people would actually call it easy.

- The forward loop is like a forward roll through the air—while holding on to a windsurfer, with your feet in the footstraps. In fact, really expert riders sometimes take a foot out of the footstraps partway through the loop.

WHEN ARE CONDITIONS BEST?

Beginners: In the morning, there are lighter winds, so conditions are great for beginners in the sheltered parts of the bay.

Intermediate sailors and experts: Around lunchtime, the wind starts to increase. This happens because the desert behind the town gets hotter, pulling cool air off the sea and strengthening the wind. The effect is especially strong during the summer, when the sun is hottest.

Tip from a Local
Essaouira is famous for its pottery—it's fun to explore the winding streets of the Safi area, where many potters have small shops.

Tiree Wave Classic

TIREE WAVE CLASSIC
Location: Tiree, Scotland
Type of sailing: wave sailing
Difficulty level: 5 of 5
Contest held: October

Every October, the little ferry that travels to the tiny Scottish island of Tiree gets suddenly busy. The deck is unusually crowded, covered in campers and cars loaded up with brightly colored windsurfing gear. The passengers are on their way to one of the longest-running wave-sailing contests around—the Tiree Wave Classic.

With so many good sailors around, finding a bit of air space for your loop can be tricky.

A BIT OF HISTORY

The Tiree Wave Classic was first held back in 1986. The event soon began to attract some of the world's best windsurfers. By 2007, the Wave Classic had become so successful that it became part of the World Cup, windsurfing's top level of competition.

WHY TIREE?

What is it that makes the world's best windsurfers willing to make the long trek up to Scotland's Western Isles? After all, most of them are used to warm seas and palm trees on the beach—not the chilly conditions of Scotland in October.

Competitors head out for the start of one of the wave-sailing contests at the Tiree Classic.

Tiree has three big attractions for windsurfers:
- The average wind speed is 16.8 miles per hour (27 kilometers per hour).
- In autumn, spring and winter, big surf rolls in from the Atlantic.
- The island gets the most sunshine of anywhere in the United Kingdom, and has long, beautiful white-sand beaches. The water is so blue that you could imagine you're in the Caribbean (until your teeth start chattering).

Ho'okipa

Ho'okipa is a name that puts equal feelings of fear and excitement into the hearts of windsurfers the world over. Everyone who sails here has a story to tell—of half their equipment being smashed to pieces on the rocks, perhaps, or of the wind dying as a **set** of giant waves comes into view. This is not a place for the fainthearted.

HO'OKIPA
Location: Maui, Hawaii
Type of sailing: wave sailing
Difficulty level: 5 of 5
Best season: March to May and September to November

Tip from a Local
Unless you are an expert sailor, the place to head on Maui is Kanaha, where the sheltered lagoon is great for all levels.

WHY HO'OKIPA?
Expert windsurfers come to Ho'okipa for one reason: the wave sailing. In spring and autumn, trade winds blow steadily and mast-high waves roll on to the reef. These conditions create a wave-sailor's playground. There are many hazards, though: sharp lava rocks, **rip currents**, and sudden drops in the wind in the area where waves break.

Hot wave-riding action from Ho'okipa, Hawaii.

If you like Ho'okipa ...

you could also try:
• Margaret River, Western Australia
• Le Morne, Mauritrius
• Ponta Preta, Cape Verde
They all offer extreme wave-sailing action.

Wave riding etiquette

WHEN ARE CONDITIONS BEST?

Beginners and intermediate sailors: Ho'okipa is not for sailors in these categories. Intermediates who are confident might be able to sail along the coast at Spreckelsville, but even here the standard is usually very, very high.

Experts: The best times of year for big surf and trade winds are spring and autumn.

However you look at it, this is going to hurt. You have to be brave to sail at Ho'okipa.

Riding a windsurfing board in big waves is a dangerous business. Sailors have developed a set of rules to help make sure everyone stays as safe as possible:

• Sailors heading out through the waves have right of way. Someone surfing in, toward the beach, has to steer around them.

• One sailor per wave. If someone else is already riding a wave, let him or her have it, and look for another one.

• If more than one sailor tries to catch a wave, the upwind sailor (the one closest to where the wind is blowing from) has the right to ride the wave.

• Always be aware of other people in the water—sailors, surfers, kayakers and swimmers, for example—and make sure you steer a wide path around them.

THE SECRET LANGUAGE OF WINDSURFING

set group of waves that appear one after another, close together

rip current strong ocean current, caused when water pushed ashore by waves flows back out to sea

Glossary

across the wind at 90 degrees to the wind direction

blasting windsurfing at maximum speed

boom rail attached to the mast, which the sailor holds on to

deck top of a windsurfing board

flat-water sailing windsurfing on a lake or ocean with little or no waves

freestyle using jumps, fast turns, and spins of the sail

jibe turn with the nose of the board away from the wind

kitesurfing water sport powered by a kite, with the sailor standing on a small, surfboard-like board

kook incompetent person

mast foot attachment between the mast and the deck

rig sail, mast, and boom together

rip current strong ocean current, caused when water pushed ashore by waves flows back out to sea

sailor someone who does windsurfing or other kinds of sailing

set group of waves that appear one after another, close together

sheet in pull the trailing end of the boom toward the board

sheet out release the trailing edge of the boom so that the sail catches less wind

swell rolling ocean waves that come into the beach in lines

tack turn with the nose of the board into the wind

uphaul rope attached to boom, used to pull sail from water

wave sailing windsurfing on rough water, particularly on ocean waves

wind chop small, peaky waves thrown up by wind

OTHER WORDS WINDSURFERS USE

clew corner of the sail farthest from the mast

leech imaginary straight line from the tip of the sail to the clew

leeward the side away from the wind

luffing flapping of the sail when the mast edge is pointing too much into the wind

newbie person who is new to windsurfing

offshore wind wind blowing away from the shore; dangerous for sailors, as it blows them out to sea

onshore wind wind blowing toward the shore

sea breeze wind that happens in the afternoon on hot days. As the land heats up, the warm air above it rises. Cooler air from above the sea rushes in to take its place, causing an onshore wind.

sideshore wind blowing across the shore

windward the side facing the wind

Finding out More

THE INTERNET

FactHound offers a safe, fun way to find Internet sites related to this book. All of the sites on FactHound have been researched by our staff.

Here's all you do:
Visit www.facthound.com
FactHound will fetch the best sites for you!

BOOKS

Radical Sports: Windsurfing Amanda Barker (Heinemann Library, 2000)

X-Treme Sports: Windsurfing Bob Italia and Stephanie F. Hedlund (Checkerboard Books, 2003)

Each of these children's books introduces the basic skills and techniques of windsurfing for beginners and gives advice about equipment and clothing.

Windsurfing: The Essential Guide to Equipment and Techniques Simon Bornhoft (New Holland Publishers, 2004)
Although this is a book for adults as well as children, it is reasonably easy to follow. The author is a former top-level windsurfer, and has been a successful windsurfing coach for over 20 years.

MAGAZINE

Wind Surfing is one of the leading windsurfing magazines in the United States. It includes equipment tests, interviews, and other news, and takes a wider-ranging view than some other magazines, with articles from North America, Europe, and the rest of the world. The magazine has a website at **www.windsurfingmag.com.**

Index

Albeau, Antoine 13

barrel rolls 25
blasting 10, 11, 20
board types 5

Cabarete, Dominican
   Republic 8–9
   hurricane season 8
carving jibes 21
Cervantes, Australia 18
Columbia River Gorge,
   Washington/Oregon,
   USA 20–21

Dahab, Egypt 16–17
Deseado Estuary, Argentina
   25
Diethelm, Patrik 13

El Yaque, Venezuela 18–19
Essaouira, Morocco 24–25
etiquette 29

Foca, Turkey 14
footstraps 19, 21, 25
Forest Beach Park, Illinois,
   USA 7
"French Trench," France 13

harness 5, 19
hauling up the sail 9, 14
Ho'okipa, Hawaii, USA
   28–29
Hydroptère 13

jibing 14, 15, 21
jumps 4, 9, 14, 17, 18, 23,
   25

Kanaha, Hawaii, USA 28
Kilifi, Kenya 8
kitesurfing 10, 12, 13, 22

Lake Arenal, Costa Rica
   14–15
Lake Garda, Italy 6–7
Le Morne, Mauritius 29
Lesvos, Greece 11
Levante wind, Spain 22,
   23
loops 25, 26
Lüderitz Speed Challenge,
   Namibia 13

Margaret River, Australia
   29
Maynard, Finian 13

Ora wind, Italy 7

Paracuru, Brazil 23
planing 16, 17, 19, 21
Poniente wind, Spain 22,
   23
Ponta Preta, Cape Verde
   29
Poole Harbour, England
   10–11
Porto Heli, Greece 16

rip currents 28, 29
River Rhine, Germany 20

sail sizes 5, 12, 19
sailing types
   flat water 6, 8, 10, 11, 14,
      15, 16, 17,
   freestyle 18, 19
   slalom 5
   speed 5, 12–13
   wave 8, 9, 11, 16, 17, 24,
      26, 27, 28, 29
Saintes-Maries-de-la-Mer,
   France 13
Sandbanks, England 10, 11
sheeting in 21, 23
sheeting out 23
speed sailing world records 13
Speed World Cup 12–13
steering 11
surfing 10, 19
Swell City, Washington, USA
   20, 21

tacking 14, 15
Tarifa, Spain 22–23
Tiree Wave Classic, Scotland
   26–27
Torbole, Lake Garda, Italy 7
turning around 15

Walvis Bay Speed Week,
   Namibia 13
wetsuit 7, 8, 22
wind chop 18